Outline

1. The Work of Jesus Continues with the Apostles (1:1–11)
2. The Mission in Jerusalem (1:12–8:3)
   a. The ministry of Peter (1:12–5:42)
   b. The ministry of Stephen (6:1–8:3)
3. The Mission in Samaria and Judea (8:4–11:18)
   a. The ministry of Philip (8:4–40)
   b. The conversion of Saul (Paul) (9:1–31)
   c. The ministry of Peter continues (9:32–11:18)
4. The Mission to the Ends of the Earth (11:19–28:31)
   a. The ministry of Barnabas (11:19–30)
   b. The conclusion of Peter's ministry (12:1–19a)
   c. The death of Herod Agrippa I (12:19b–25)
   d. The ministry of Paul and Barnabas: First missionary journey (13:1–14:28)
   e. The Jerusalem Council (15:1–35)
   f. The ministry of Paul and Silas: Second missionary journey (15:36–18:22)
   g. The ministry of Paul: Third missionary journey (18:23–21:14)
   h. Paul in Jerusalem (21:15–23:10)
   i. Paul in Caesarea (23:11–26:32)
   j. Paul taken to Rome (27:1–28:29)
   k. Conclusion: The gospel preached throughout the world (28:30–31)

TIME LINE OF THE BOOK OF ACTS

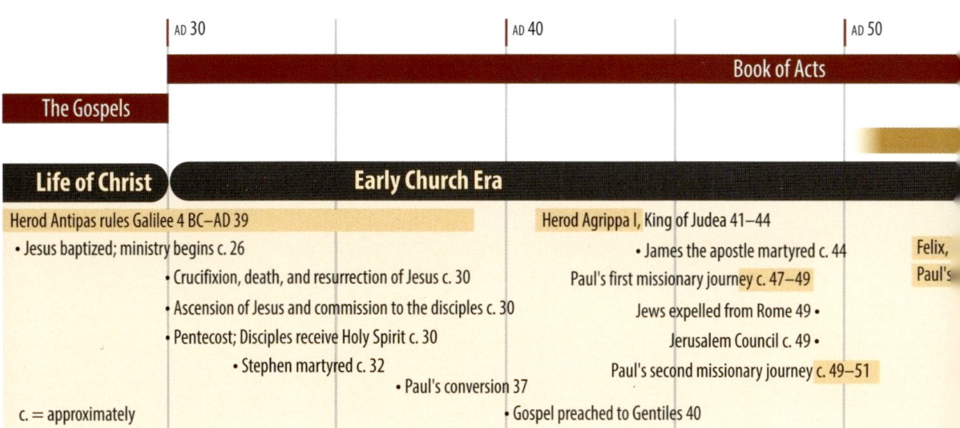

Paul's Missionary Journeys

JOURNEY	ACTS	BASIC INFORMATION	HIGHLIGHTS
First Journey AD 47–49	13:1–14:28	**Travelers:** Paul, Barnabas, John Mark **Main Route:** (Modern names) Cyprus and Turkey **Distance:** 1,400 miles	After being set apart for this journey, Paul and Barnabas faced a sorcerer, opposition from Jewish leaders, sick people who were healed, persecutions, and the crucial Jerusalem Council at the end of the journey (15:1–35).
Second Journey AD 49–51	15:36–18:22	**Travelers:** Paul, Silas, Timothy, Priscilla and Aquilla, Luke **Main Route:** (Modern names) Syria, Turkey, Greece, Jerusalem **Distance:** 2,800 miles	Paul and Barnabas went separate ways. With Silas, Paul visited churches, and received visions from God. They were thrown in jail and met people who eagerly received their message. At Athens, Paul preached to the Greeks.
Third Journey AD 52–57	18:23–21:16	**Travelers:** Paul, Timothy, Luke, others **Main Route:** (Modern names) Turkey, Greece, Lebanon, Israel **Distance:** 2,700 miles	Paul visited the churches of the area. He remained for two years at Ephesus. Paul wrote several of his letters during this journey. He revived a young man who had an accident. He also experienced persecution and suffering. At the end, he went to Jerusalem.
Journey to Rome AD 57–62	21:17–28:31	**Travelers:** Paul, Roman guards, Luke, others **Main Route:** (Modern names) Israel, Lebanon, Turkey, Crete, Malta, Sicily, Italy **Distance:** 2,250 miles	Paul was arrested in Jerusalem. In Caesarea, Paul was tried before two governors: Felix and Festus. After two years, Paul appealed to Caesar and appeared before King Agrippa. Paul was sent to Rome. After a shipwrecked trip, Paul arrived in Rome. He remained there under house arrest for two years.

Our History and Heritage

The book of Acts is not simply ancient history. It is our story, the story that informs who we are. We are God's people, called to be witnesses of what God did and continues to do in Jesus. By studying and understanding the way God acted in history, we become more attuned to the ways God is active among us today. God is active, as the book of Acts shows. We must be sensitive to the way the Spirit moves in our midst and in the world to join in the mission.

The Scriptures do not promise that the mission is easy and painless. To the contrary, being Jesus' disciples implies danger and opposition. But the stories in the book of Acts show that Jesus is faithful to his promise to be with us always. The stories inspire us to be brave and obedient. The end of the book of Acts represents only the beginning of the church's life and mission: "[Paul] proclaimed the kingdom of God and taught about the Lord Jesus Christ—with all boldness and without hindrance!" (Acts 28:31).

THE SPREAD OF CHRISTIANITY IN THE FIRST CENTURY AD

THE MISSION TO THE GENTILES

- Jesus' disciples continued to preach the gospel outside of Jerusalem, reaching places like Joppa (9:42), Caesarea (10), Phoenicia, Cyprus, and Antioch (11:19). Antioch became the base for Paul's missionary journeys.
- Despite persecution, Jesus' followers continued to preach the gospel in and around Jerusalem so that "the word of God continued to spread and flourish" (12:24).
- Along with Barnabas, Paul began an adventure that would take him to Asia Minor, the Greek Islands, and beyond. He rarely traveled alone. Barnabas was his first companion (15:39–40). Silas would be his next companion (15:40). Along the way, other companions joined the apostle in his journeys.

The Gospel in the Book of Acts

This basic outline was helpful for Christians then and is helpful for Christians today.

1. God's promises to Israel are now fulfilled with the coming of Jesus, the Messiah (2:30; 3:19, 24; 10:43; 26:6–7, 22).
2. God anointed Jesus as the Messiah during his baptism (10:38).
3. Jesus began his ministry in Galilee after his baptism (10:37). His ministry showed God's power with words and actions.
4. Jesus, the Messiah, suffered and died on the cross according to God's own plan (2:23; 3:13–15, 18; 4:11; 10:39; 26:23).
5. God raised Jesus from the dead. Jesus appeared to his disciples (2:24, 31–32; 3:15, 26; 10:40–41; 17:31; 26:23).
6. God exalted Jesus and gave him the name of "Lord" (2:25–29, 33–36; 3:13; 10:36).
7. God sent the Holy Spirit to create a new community, the church (1:8; 2:14–18, 38–39; 10:44–47).
8. Jesus will come back one day to judge all people and to make all things new (3:20–21; 10:42; 17:31).
9. The good news of Jesus is for all people. The gospel urges all people to hear the message, repent, and be baptized (2:21, 38; 3:19; 10:43, 47–48; 17:30; 26:20).

THE AUTHOR

An early and reliable church tradition names Luke as the author of Acts and the Gospel of Luke. Because of the historical sequence found in the Gospel of Luke and Acts, it is likely that Acts was written after the Gospel. If Luke wrote the Gospel around the years AD 60–62, it is likely that Acts was written shortly after that period. Luke was one of the apostle Paul's companions during his last three journeys.

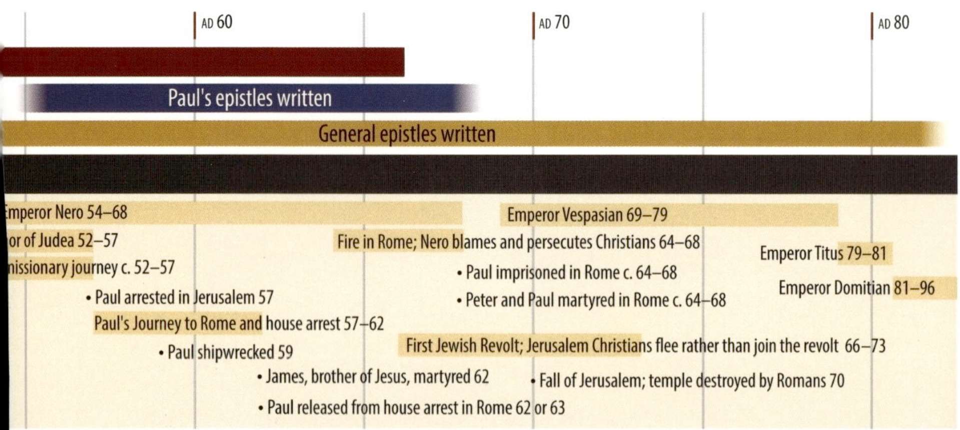

The Good News

We learn about the good news the apostles were to share from their own speeches.

- There are 24 speeches in the book of Acts.
- However, only eight of them help us with learning about the content of the gospel message:
  - Six of them are speeches addressed to a Jewish audience (2:14–39; 3:12–26; 4:8– 12; 5:29–32; 10:34–43; 13:16–41)
  - Two of them to a Gentile audience (14:15–17; 17:22–34).

Examples:

SPEECH	AUDIENCE	REFERENCE	FOCUS OF THE CONTENT
Peter's speech to the other disciples in the upper room	Christians	1:16–26	· Fulfillment of God's purpose in Scripture (16, 20) · Activity of the Holy Spirit (16) · Decision to replace Judas (24)
Peter's speech to the crowd in Jerusalem on Pentecost	Jewish not-yet believers	2:14–39	· God's actions as fulfilling his promises in Joel (16–21) · God's actions and acceptance of Jesus' life, death and resurrection (22–24) · Conclusion: God made Jesus Lord and Messiah (36)
Peter's speech to Cornelius's household in Caesarea	Gentile not-yet believers	10:34–43	· God shows no partiality (34) · Jesus' preaching came from God (35) · God anointed Jesus with the Holy Spirit (38) · God raised Jesus from the dead (40) · The apostles as witnesses to these events (41) · God appointed Jesus as judge (42)
Paul's speech at the Areopagus in Athens	Pagans	17:22–34	· God has revealed himself (23) · God is creator and sustainer of the world (24–25) · God is the Lord of all nations (26) · God wants people to seek and find him (27–28) · Idolatry misses the mark (29) · God calls all to repentance (30) · God appointed Jesus as judge by raising him from the dead (31–32)

leaders. His letters, which form the bulk of the New Testament and are aimed at instructing and guiding those new groups and leaders, continue to shape, inform, and nurture the faith of millions of believers today all over the world.

THE MISSION IN JERUSALEM

- After Jesus ascended to heaven (1:8), the disciples received the Holy Spirit on Pentecost (2:1–4).
- Peter preached and 3,000 people received the gospel (2:5–41).
- The apostles Peter and John performed miracles (3:1–10) and preached the gospel in the temple in Jerusalem and 5,000 people believed (3:11–4:4).
- Despite the persecution against the disciples, many people believed in the gospel. The apostles chose seven believers "full of the Spirit and wisdom" (6:3) to help them with the life of the growing group of believers.

THE MISSION IN JUDEA AND SAMARIA

- In the midst of persecution, Christ's disciples continued to proclaim the good news. Stephen, one of the seven chosen by the apostles, provided an example of perseverance, faith, and obedience when he faced an angry crowd. He preached a powerful message, the longest speech in the book, and argued for the gospel using the Old Testament as his basis. Stephen became the first recorded martyr (6:8–7:60). Saul, a Jewish leader who would later become the apostle Paul, was present at that moment.
- After Stephen's death, the persecution against believers increased dramatically and "all except the apostles were scattered throughout Judea and Samaria" (8:1). As they moved away from Jerusalem, they brought the gospel with them. Philip preached in Samaria and to the Ethiopian eunuch, who had been to Jerusalem to worship God. After his baptism, the Ethiopian official returned home, bringing along with him the transformative power of the gospel (8:26–40).
- Jesus confronted Saul on the road to Damascus (9:1–22) and called him to become his instrument "to carry my name before the Gentiles and their kings and before the people of Israel" (9:15). The church found peace throughout Judea, Galilee and Samaria and "grew in numbers" (9:31).

testimony of the resurrected Jesus (Acts 2:14–41). Peter's spiritual story led him to recognize many times his personal struggles and his surrender to God's will.

In the book of Acts, the encounter of Peter and the Roman centurion Cornelius confronted the apostle with God's broad plan for humanity. But this event also became a hinging moment in the history of the church. The renewal of all creation started on Pentecost, but the world had continued turning apparently unperturbed. The world was still divided. Jews and Gentiles were separate. But Peter's vision in Acts 10 changed everything.

A Roman Centurion—it would be equivalent to the rank of captain in today's armies—Cornelius was "devout and God-fearing" (10:2). God revealed himself in a vision to Cornelius (10:3–8). God also gave Peter a vision of the "unclean" animals. These were ritually unclean animals not fit for consumption according to the law (Lev. 11). The point of this vision is clear: "Do not call anything impure that God has made clean" (10:15). For many Jews at that time, the impurity of those animals was equivalent to the impurity of the Gentiles. God was preparing Peter for the next phase of the mission: the gospel for the Gentiles.

The conclusion of the story is remarkable: after hearing Peter's presentation of the gospel (10:34–43), "the Holy Spirit came on all who heard the message" (10:44). God was putting his seal of approval and welcoming on the Gentiles. Peter understood what God was doing. He said, "Surely no one can stand in the way of their being baptized with water" (10:47). As he explained his actions in Jerusalem, Peter concludes, "So then, even to Gentiles God has granted repentance that leads to life" (11:18).

The Apostle Paul and the Mission

Before becoming Paul, Saul was a deadly enemy of Christianity. After a personal encounter with the resurrected Christ (9:1–19), Paul became God's special representative to the Gentiles. His ministry, as recorded in the book of Acts, changed the history of the church and of the world. In four recorded trips, Paul preached the gospel from Jerusalem to Philippi, Athens, Corinth, Ephesus, Rome, and back to Jerusalem. He planted new churches and trained new

These presentations to different audiences show us the importance of allowing our message today to be adapted to different audiences. Although every person needs to hear and accept the message of the gospel, we must allow our presentation of the gospel to take different forms for different people. However, the message of the gospel is the same.

THE MAIN CHARACTERS

The book of Acts is a story. The focus of this story is God. In the book, we learn what God did in the early life of the church.

God: The Center of the Christian Story

The central character in the book is God. The book of Acts tells us the story of God in relation to the community of followers of Christ, the early church. We learn about God from the different relationships within the book. From the book we learn that:

- God is Creator and greater than the temple (7:48–50).
- He enables people to be his followers (2; 4:24–29).
- He is the God of Israel's ancestors (3:13; 22:14; 24:14).
- He is the God of the Gentiles (10:45; 11:18; 15:7–9, 14; 21:19–20).
- He is the God of history and will accomplish his purposes.

In the book of Acts, we encounter the same God of grace and mercy we find in the Old Testament. He has taken the initiative to rescue his people, as he had promised he would, and extends the invitation to all the nations.

WHO WAS THEOPHILUS?

Both Luke and Acts address a man named Theophilus (Luke 1:3; Acts 1:1). He is addressed as "most excellent," a common way of addressing socially important people.

Books were expensive, and only a few people and groups were able to afford them. It was common to write books for a wealthy patron who would keep them and grant access to others to read. If Theophilus was wealthy, then it is possible that he financed Luke's writing, paid for copies of the books, and granted churches access to the books.

Acts was meant for several audiences: first, the book is addressed to an individual—Theophilus; second, it was for other people like him—perhaps Romans who were intrigued by Christianity; and third, it's for all Christian believers—Jews and Gentiles alike.

Jesus: The Kingdom of God and the Mission

We learn about God by knowing Jesus Christ. As the epistle to the Hebrews teaches us, " ... in these last days he has spoken to us by his Son ... " (Heb. 1:2). If the Old Testament reveals God, the New Testament perfects that revelation in the person of Jesus. We learn much about Jesus from the speeches in the book of Acts. We learn that Jesus is:

- The Promised Messiah (2:36; 3:20; 5:42; 8:5; 17:3; 18:5)
- Son of David (2:30; 13:23)
- Lord (2:36; 10:36)
- Son of God (9:20; 13:33)
- Prophet like Moses (3:22–23; 7:37)
- Servant of the Lord (3:13, 26; 4:30; 8:32–33)
- Son of Man (7:56)
- The righteous one (3:14; 7:52; 22:14)
- The author of life (3:15)
- Leader and Savior (5:31)
- One destined to suffer (3:18; 17:3; 26:23)
- Rejected (2:23–24; 3:13–15; 8:32–33; 13:28)

THE HOLY SPIRIT

- The Spirit is involved in the works of God:
  - Creation (Ps. 104:30)
  - Incarnation (Matt. 1:18; Luke 1:35)
  - Resurrection (Rom. 1:4; 8:11)
  - Salvation (John 15:26; 16:8; Rom. 8:14–17)
  - Christian Life (John 16:13; Rom. 8:26–27; 15:18–19; 1 Cor. 2:10; Gal. 5:22–23)
- The Spirit is a person:
  - He can be lied to (Acts 5:3–4)
  - He can be grieved (Eph. 4:30)
  - He has a name (Matt. 28:19).
- The Spirit is God (Acts 5:3; 1 Cor. 3:16; 12:4–6; 2 Peter 1:21)

At the center of the apostolic message we find Jesus. Jesus is presented as God's ultimate solution for all humanity, Jews and Gentiles alike. In all of it, Jesus is presented as representing God and carrying on God's plans for humanity. Jesus makes it possible for God's mission to save his creation to be fulfilled. Consistently throughout the book, Jesus is presented as Lord. As Lord, he sent his followers as ambassadors to carry on his will, to spread the good news that the kingdom of God had arrived.

The Leaders of the Mission

Most of the book deals with how Jesus' followers carry on God's mission. The challenges that the apostles faced teach us that Jesus is faithful and his presence and protection is with his people.

Rather than a detailed account of the ministry of all the disciples, the text concentrates on two strong leaders: the apostles Peter and Paul. Their stories illustrate well the task and challenges of the mission. They also illustrate the ways the Holy Spirit has equipped us to fulfill our calling.

ACTION	PETER	PAUL
Healed a lame man	3:2–8	14:8–10
Performed a miracle at a distance	5:15	19:12
Exorcised evil spirits	5:16	19:12
Defeated sorcerers	8:18–24	13:6–11
Raised the dead	9:36–43	20:9–12
Defended themselves against Jewish authorities	4:8–12; 5:27–32	23:3–21; 23:1–6; 28:25–28
Received heavenly visions	10:9–16	16:9
Present when the Spirit came upon new believers	8:14–17	19:1–7
Miraculously released from prison	5:19; 12:7–11	16:25–27
Proclaimed the same message	2:27	13:35

THE MISSION TO THE WORLD

The starting point of the mission was Jerusalem. Slowly, the Holy Spirit pushed the apostles away from Jerusalem to Judea, Samaria and to all the nations. This outward movement shows God's desire to reach all peoples on earth. The stories of the mission work of the apostolic church are powerful and inspirational. They not only show the faithfulness and determination of the apostles, but, more importantly, they show God's guiding and protecting hand. It is God's mission, as the early refrain in the book reminds us: "And the Lord added to their number day by day those who were being saved" (Acts 2:47).

The Apostle Peter and the Mission

The apostle Peter had an exceptional spiritual journey. He became one of the first disciples Jesus called (Matt. 4:18). He was a leader among the disciples during and after Jesus' ministry on earth. After Pentecost, Peter was the first to bring

GOD'S COMMUNITY IS CHARACTERIZED BY:

Baptism. The powerful symbolism of baptism shapes the character and identity of the church. People in this new community are those who die and are born again, empowered and sealed by the Spirit. This is a new identity; there is no longer Gentile or Jew, or any other social or biological characteristic that separates them. They are all united as one body.

Worship. Worship is a visual declaration of our deepest beliefs. In worship, we express with our whole beings what is most important to us. Worship is also a humbling experience where we recognize our ultimate dependence on God. Worship shapes this new community.

Fellowship. The life of the new community was central to their message. This community is characterized by an intimate fellowship with other believers and with the Lord. Fellowship with other believers flows from our fellowship with God. In the breaking of bread, which most likely included the Lord's Supper, fellowship became a central part of that community.

Instruction. The church is apostolic because it is founded on the teachings of the apostles. They taught all that Jesus had taught them and what the Spirit revealed to them. The church is God's initiative. The church is an extension of her Lord.

Mission. The main reason for the existence of the church is God's mission. Through her life and spoken testimony, God would spread the kingdom of God. A kingdom that was already active but not yet completely here. The church is God's active representative on earth.

Stephen: The First Christian Martyr

Stephen was one of the seven men the church chose and the apostles ordained to serve alongside them. Stephen became a leader of the early church, "a man full of God's grace and power, performed great wonders and signs among the people" (Acts 6:8). His speech before the religious leaders of the Jews caused an angry response that led to Stephen's death. Jesus had warned the disciples, "If they persecuted me, they will persecute you also" (John 15:20). However, Jesus promised that when persecution occurred, the Holy Spirit would be present encouraging and strengthening believers (John 14:16; 15:26). The story of Stephen shows the strength, conviction, and faithfulness that is possible through the power of the Spirit.

The Church

As the number of believers grew, the book of Acts summarizes the life of this new community: "They devoted themselves to the apostles' teaching and to fellowship, to the breaking of bread and to prayer. Everyone was filled with awe at the many wonders and signs performed by the apostles" (2:42–43).

This emphasis on the mission can be best seen in the movement of God in Luke and Acts:

- God invades planet earth from the outside in as a baby (Luke 1:5–4:13).
- Jesus invades Galilee of the Gentiles first (Luke 4:14–9:50).
- Jesus invades Samaria and Judea (Luke 9:51–19:27).
- Jesus invades Jerusalem at Passover (Luke 19:28–22:46).

CRUCIFIXION AND RESURRECTION (Luke 22:47–Acts 1:11).

- The Holy Spirit takes Jerusalem at Pentecost (Acts 1:12–7:60).
- The Holy Spirit takes Judea and Samaria (Acts 8:1–40).
- The Holy Spirit takes the nations (Acts 9:1–28:31).
- The Holy Spirit takes the world from the inside out through the body of Christ.

ROSE PUBLISHING

Published by Rose Publishing
an imprint of Tyndale House Ministries

www.hendricksonrose.com

Author: Benjamin Galan, MTS, ThM

Printed in the United States of America. 080821SCG

RELIGION/Biblical Studies/New Testament

ISBN 978-1-59636-738-8

9 781596 367388

257X *Book of Acts*
Retailers: Package of 5 pamphlets = ISBN: 9781596367395